I WONDER Why

Greeks Built Temples

and other questions
about ancient
Greece

Fiona Macdonald

KINGFISHER
NEW YORK

KINGFISHER
LONDON & NEW YORK

Copyright © Kingfisher 2012
Published in the United States by Kingfisher,
175 Fifth Ave., New York, NY 10010
Kingfisher is an imprint of Macmillan Children's Books,
London.
All rights reserved.

First published in 1997 by Kingfisher
This edition published 2012 by Kingfisher

Distributed in the U.S. and Canada by Macmillan,
175 Fifth Ave., New York, NY 10010

Library of Congress Cataloging-in-Publication data
has been applied for.

ISBN 978-0-7534-6706-0 (HC)
ISBN 978-0-7534-6705-3 (PB)

Kingfisher books are available for special promotions and
premiums. For details contact: Special Markets Department,
Macmillan, 175 Fifth Ave., New York, NY 10010.

For more information, please visit www.kingfisherbooks.com

Printed in China
9 8 7 6 5 4 3 2 1
1TR/1011/WKT/UG/140MA

Illustrations: Simone Boni (Virgil Pomfret) 26–27; Peter Dennis
(Linda Rogers) 8–9, 14–15, 24–25; Chris Forsey cover; Terry
Gabbey (AFA Ltd.) 18–19; Luigi Galante (Virgil Pomfret) 6–7,
16–17; Ian Jackson 22–23, 30–31; Tony Kenyon (B. L. Kearley)
all cartoons; Nicki Palin 20–21, 28–29; Claudia Saraceni
12–13; Thomas Trojer 10–11; Richard Ward 4–5.

CONTENTS

Who were the ancient Greeks?

The ancient Greeks were people who lived in Greece from around 3,500 years ago. But they didn't live only in Greece. Some lived to the north and the east, in lands that we now call Bulgaria and Turkey. Others lived on small, rocky islands in the Aegean Sea.

Many Greek people set sail for North Africa, Turkey, Italy, and France. They found safe harbors, where they built new homes and towns, and cleared the land for farming.

Greek homeland
Greek colonies
FRANCE
ITALY
TURKEY
Aegean Sea
NORTH AFRICA
Mediterranean Sea

By 500 B.C., the Greek world was large, rich, and powerful. It stretched from France in the west to Turkey in the east.

Wherever they went, the Greek settlers took their own way of life. They must have looked odd to the locals!

The Greeks were a talented people. They had good laws and strong armies. They built beautiful temples and theaters. And they were great thinkers, artists, and athletes.

Why did Greece grow bigger and bigger?

Greece and its homelands were small, and much of its land was too rocky for farming. By about 750 B.C., there was little room left for new towns or farms, and food began to run short. Because of this, many people left Greece to look for new places to live, and the Greek world began to grow.

Was Greece one big, happy country?

Each state was made up of a city and the surrounding countryside. Many city-states lay close to the sea and had a harbor, too.

Ancient Greece was not a single country like Greece is today. It was made up of different states that were cut off from one another by high mountains, deep valleys, or the sea. The states weren't much bigger than cities, but they each had their own laws and army and often fought with one another. Athens was the biggest city-state.

HARBOR

TEMPLE

PRISON

AGORA
(MARKETPLACE)

SCHOOL

CITY WALLS

FARMLAND

Where did the citizens take charge?

Sparta was a city-state in southern Greece. It was ruled by two kings from two royal families, who were helped by a council of wise old men.

In Athens, all grown men who weren't slaves were citizens. They could choose their government officials and vote for or against new laws. Citizens could also speak at the Assembly. This was a huge open-air meeting where people stood up and told the government what it should be doing.

EATER

HOUSES

There had to be at least 6,000 citizens at every Assembly. They all met on the slopes of a hill in Athens and voted by raising one hand.

Most wealthy Greek households had slaves. The slaves did all of the hard work, such as building, farming, housework, and taking care of the children.

Where did the clock go drip-drop?

Citizens who spoke at the Assembly weren't allowed to drone on for too long. Each speaker was timed with a water clock. When the last drop of water had dripped out of the jar, the speaker's time was up. He had to sit down and hold his tongue!

Who were the fiercest soldiers?

The soldiers of Sparta were the fiercest army in ancient Greece. They were brave, ruthless, and very well trained. None of the men had ordinary jobs, even in peacetime. They spent their whole lives just training and fighting.

Spartan warriors were famous for their long, flowing hair. Before a battle, they sat down and combed it. Perhaps their long manes made them feel like fierce lions!

For Spartans, bravery was more important than anything else. To punish cowards, they shaved off half their hair and half their beard! This was a terrible disgrace.

Who paid for weapons and armor?

Greek soldiers fought side by side in tight rows called phalanxes. Each soldier's shield overlapped his neighbor's, making a strong wall of shields that protected all of the soldiers.

Greek soldiers had to buy their own weapons and armor. A wealthy soldier bought himself a sharp spear and sword, a strong shield, and expensive body armor. But a poor soldier made do with whatever he could find. And sometimes this was little more than an animal skin and a wooden club!

In Sparta, it wasn't just the men who had to be in shape. Women had to do lots of exercises to make sure their babies were healthy and strong.

After winning a battle, soldiers sometimes gave their armor to the gods as a thank-you present. They placed it inside a temple or hung it on the branches of a tree.

Why did ships have long noses?

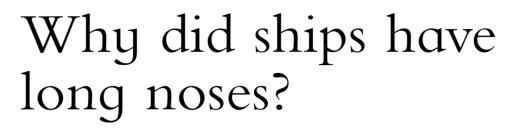

Greek warships had a long, sharp spike at the front. It was called a ram, and in battle it could be deadly. The oarsmen rowed as fast as they could toward an enemy ship and tried to smash a hole in its side with the ram. With any luck, the enemy ship would sink and its crew would all be drowned.

Most Greek ships had a big eye painted on both sides of the prow. The sailors hoped that these staring eyes would frighten away evil spirits and protect the men until they were safely home.

The biggest warships were called triremes and had three rows of oarsmen along each side of the boat. With 170 men pulling on the oars, ships zipped through the water at an amazing speed.

Each ship had a flute player who piped tunes with a steady beat. The oarsmen all pulled their oars in time with the music, which meant that they didn't get tangled up!

Why was it easier to travel by sea?

There are many islands in Greece, and boats are often still the only way to get from one island to another. But the ancient Greeks used boats to get around the mainland, too. Sailing along the coast was much quicker and easier than struggling up steep, stony tracks on the back of a weary donkey!

11

Who was the goddess of wisdom?

Athena was the goddess of war and also of wisdom, and her symbol was the wise owl. She had special powers to protect the city of Athens. Because of this, the citizens loved and worshiped her. They built Athena her very own temple—the Parthenon—high on the Acropolis, a hill overlooking the city.

According to stories, the gods lived on top of Mount Olympus, the highest mountain in Greece. But they didn't always behave as you would expect gods to—they spent a lot of their time arguing!

Hermes messenger of the gods

Zeus king of the gods

Demeter goddess of crops

Aphrodite goddess of love and beauty

Hera queen of the gods; goddess of women and children

Hades god of the underworld

The Greeks believed in many different gods and goddesses. Each one had different powers. Some of the gods were kind, but others were stern and cruel.

Who told stories about the gods?

A famous poet named Homer told many exciting stories about gods and heroes. His long poem *The Odyssey* tells the adventures of Odysseus, a Greek soldier sailing home to Ithaca from the war with Troy. The sea god Poseidon tries to sink his ship, but with Athena's protection, Odysseus finally gets home.

Poseidon was the god of the sea. He tried to sink Odysseus's ship by stirring up violent storms.

Inside the Parthenon stood a towering statue of Athena—about ten times taller than you! It was covered with precious gold and ivory.

13

Who talked to the trees?

The Greeks believed that nature goddesses called dryads lived deep in the woods. Priests and priestesses guarded the holy woods and prayed to the dryads. Then they listened closely for any rustlings in the trees—which might be the nature goddesses' messages in reply!

According to legend, dryads wore crowns of leaves and danced in the woods. They also carried axes—to attack anyone who damaged their trees.

14

There were more than 40 religious holidays in Athens each year. There are paintings of these festivals on wine jars and other Greek pottery. People loved festivals. They didn't have to work and there was a lot of free food and drink.

Where did Greeks empty their wine?

Many Greeks prayed to the gods in their own homes at a special altar. They liked to offer the gods presents of food or wine. Sometimes worshipers poured a whole jar of wine over an altar. More often, they drank most of the wine themselves and gave the gods only a tiny drop!

Why did Greeks build temples?

The Greeks built temples as homes for their gods. They made the buildings as magnificent as possible, using only the finest materials and very best craftsmen so that the gods would be pleased. Elegant statues, tall columns, and painted friezes decorated the outside. Inside, the rooms were filled with treasures.

Whose fingers made their fortune?

Greek craftsmen were very skilled and made beautiful works of art. Stonemasons carved marble figures, metalworkers made statues and vases of bronze, and potters and painters made wonderful jars and flasks. Some craftsmen became rich and famous and sold their work far away as well as at home.

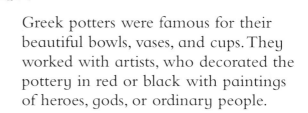

Greek potters were famous for their beautiful bowls, vases, and cups. They worked with artists, who decorated the pottery in red or black with paintings of heroes, gods, or ordinary people.

The Parthenon in Athens was built from dazzling white marble. The huge stone blocks were carried to the construction site on ox-drawn carts and pulled up to the builders on ropes and pulleys.

Greek sculptors carved wonderful statues. One story tells how the sculptor Pygmalion made such a lifelike statue of a woman that he fell in love with it! Aphrodite, the goddess of love, took pity on him and brought the statue to life.

Temple columns weren't made from one single piece of stone. They were built from drum-shaped pieces held together by pegs. The pieces fitted together snugly—as long as you put them in the right order!

17

When did a couple get married?

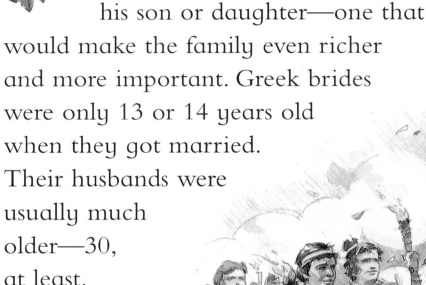

Most couples got married when their parents said so! A wealthy father wanted a good match for his son or daughter—one that would make the family even richer and more important. Greek brides were only 13 or 14 years old when they got married. Their husbands were usually much older—30, at least.

On her wedding day, a bride was driven in a chariot to her new husband's home. There was laughter and music and burning torches to light the way.

A bride's chariot was broken after her wedding as a sign that she could never go back to her old home.

18

What did girls do all day?

Young girls from wealthy families were sometimes taught how to read at home, but girls didn't go to school. Most learned from their mothers how to spin fleece into thread and then weave it into fine woolen cloth. Greek women made all of the cloth their families needed—for wall hangings, blankets, and rugs, as well as for clothes.

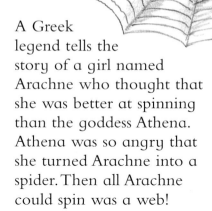

A Greek legend tells the story of a girl named Arachne who thought that she was better at spinning than the goddess Athena. Athena was so angry that she turned Arachne into a spider. Then all Arachne could spin was a web!

A few women did learn how to read and write. One of the most famous Greek poets was a woman named Sappho, who lived about 2,500 years ago.

Who went to the gym every day?

Gym is short for *gymnasium*, the Greek name for school. Boys went to school from about the age of seven. They learned the usual subjects such as reading, writing, and math, as well as how to make a speech, recite poetry, and sing.

Why were Greek clothes so comfy?

The Greeks wore light, loose-fitting clothes. There were no tight buttons or zippers, just flowing robes or simple tunics called chitons. Chitons were big squares of cloth draped over the body and held in place by pins at the shoulders and a belt around the waist.

The Greeks liked brightly colored clothes, decorated with embroidery. Most clothes were made out of wool or linen, but rich people wore silk, too.

Greek women liked to wear lots of jewelry. Wealthy women wore gold and silver bracelets, necklaces, and dangly earrings that jingled with every move.

Why were Greek shoes so bouncy?

Most Greeks liked to go barefoot at home. But when they went out, they wore cool summer sandals or warm winter boots. The comfiest ones had thick soles made of cork. This made them soft and bouncy—just right for walking on stony ground.

The Greeks wore wide-brimmed hats made of braided straw to protect themselves from the scorching summer sun.

Who took a shower in a bowl?

When the ancient Greeks wanted a shower, they undressed and crouched inside a deep pottery bowl. Then a slave would come and pour jars of cool, refreshing water over them.

Where could you buy figs, beans, cheese, and greens?

Farmers loaded their donkeys with food to sell at the agora—fruit and vegetables, cheeses, chickens, and a squealing piglet or two!

Town dwellers bought their food at the agora, the open-air market in the center of town. There was always plenty of fresh fruit, vegetables, and grains—all grown on farms just outside town. You could also buy cheeses made from goat's or sheep's milk, which were flavored with sweet-smelling herbs.

Every year, after the grape harvest, people had to jump into big wooden tubs and crush the fruit into juice to make wine. It was hot, tiring, and sticky work.

Why did farmers beat their trees?

Before farmers harvested their olives, they spread huge sheets of cloth under the trees. Then they beat the branches to make all of the ripe fruit fall on the sheets. This was much quicker and easier than trying to pick the tiny olives one by one!

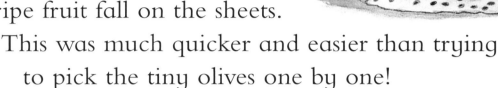

Ordinary people rarely bought meat because it was much too expensive. So when they did, they ate every scrap. They fried the lungs, stewed the intestines, and boiled the brains!

Did the Greeks get drunk at breakfast?

Certainly not! Some Greeks did drink wine at breakfast, but it was mixed with plenty of water. Most people preferred milk. Favorite breakfast foods included bread, cooked barley, eggs, fish, and figs.

Why did actors wear masks?

In ancient Greece, only boys and men were actors. They wore masks so that the audience could see what part they were playing—a man or a woman, a wise person or a fool. Greek theaters were huge, with seats for up to 17,000 people. From the back, you couldn't have seen the actors' faces, but the big, colorful masks were easy to make out.

Some plays lasted all day. The audience took cushions and rugs to put on the hard stone seats and bought snacks and wine when they felt hungry or thirsty.

Greek theaters stood on sloping hillsides. Their semicircular shape helped carry the actors' voices all the way to the back— even when they whispered!

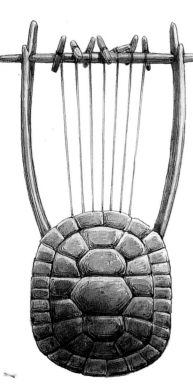

How did a tortoise make music?

Sad to say, a tortoise made music only when it was dead. An empty tortoiseshell was used to make a lyre, a musical instrument a little like a harp. Musicians attached strings to the shell and plucked them to play a tune.

The double flute was another popular musical instrument, but it was difficult to play. You needed twice as much puff as for a single flute, and each hand played a different tune.

Theater workers carried big sticks in case of trouble. Sometimes a huge audience got carried away by a play and began to riot. A few hefty whacks soon quieted them down!

Why were the Olympics held?

The Olympic Games were part of a religious festival in honor of Zeus, the king of the gods. Every four years, 20,000 people flocked to Olympia to watch athletes run, box, wrestle, and race chariots. The hardest event of all was the pentathlon. Contestants had to take part in five different sports—the long jump, running, wrestling, throwing the discus, and throwing the javelin.

Women were not allowed at the Olympics. They held their own games, in honor of Hera, the queen of the gods. The women's games had only one event, which was running.

At the Olympics, all of the athletes were naked. The Greeks were proud of their bodies and liked to show them off!

Did the winners get medals?

Winning at the Olympics was a great honor, just as it is today. But there were no medals at the ancient games. Instead, the winners got crowns made of laurel leaves, jars of olive oil, beautiful pots or vases, and pieces of wool, silk, or linen to make into clothes.

Greek boxers didn't wear padded gloves like boxers today. They simply wrapped strips of leather around their fists.

Who ran the first marathon?

In 490 B.C., the Greeks won a battle at Marathon, about 26 miles (42km) from Athens. A Greek soldier named Pheidippides ran all the way to Athens to tell the citizens the good news. Sadly, his "marathon" exhausted him, and the poor man collapsed and died.

There was no marathon race in the ancient games, but there is today. It measures 26 miles (42km)—exactly the same distance that poor Pheidippides ran 2,500 years ago.

27

Why did doctors ask so many questions?

Greek doctors were clean, well dressed, and cheerful. It made their patients trust them, and the doctors knew this helped people get better more quickly.

Greek doctors knew it was important to find out as much as they could about their patients. So they asked them all sorts of questions—what kind of food they ate, whether they got any exercise, and so on. People had once believed that illness was a punishment from the gods, but Greek doctors had more scientific ideas.

Who had his best ideas in the bathtub?

Archimedes was a mathematician who lived in Greece around 250 B.C. One day when he was taking a bath, he finally figured out a problem that had been troubling him for a long time. He was so excited that he jumped out of the bathtub shouting, "Eureka!" ("I've found it!") and ran down the street to tell his friends!

The Greeks loved learning about new ideas. They would sit under a shady tree and talk for hours about all sorts of things, from the way people lived to the future of the world.

Who discovered that Earth is round?

Greek scientists were very interested in Earth and space. In about 470 B.C., a scientist named Parmenides was watching an eclipse of the Moon. He noticed that Earth cast a dark, curved shadow on the Moon and figured out that if the shadow was curved, then Earth must be round!

One famous Greek thinker was named Diogenes. He lived in an old wooden barrel so people could see that he didn't care about money or possessions. He was interested only in ideas.

How do we know about ancient Greece?

All sorts of things have survived from ancient Greece—not just buildings and statues but also writings, weapons, jewelry, and coins. Historians study these things carefully. They look for clues to piece together a picture of the past, just as detectives look for clues in a case.

Greek pottery tells us a lot about life in ancient Greece. It's decorated with pictures of families at home, athletes, festivals, and people at work. Can you guess what job the man on this plate did?

The Greek world began to break up around 300 B.C. In Italy, the Romans were growing stronger. They invaded Greece in 148 B.C. and soon took control.

Who copied the Greeks?

About 2,000 years ago, the Romans marched into Greece. They conquered its armies and added its lands to their own empire. But Roman people respected the Greek way of life. They admired Greek poetry, plays, buildings, and art. They copied many Greek ideas and used them to improve their own way of life.

The Acropolis is a high, rocky hill in the center of Athens. Climb to the top and you're at the heart of ancient Greece. Beautiful buildings stand all around you, including the Parthenon—the temple built for the goddess Athena between 447 B.C. and 432 B.C.

Greek temples have survived for almost 2,500 years. But today they are being damaged by air pollution, which attacks the stone and eats it away.

Index